MOM

A BOOK ABOUT MOM

WITH WORDS AND PICTURES BY

me

Illustrations by Irena Freitas

WORKMAN PUBLISHING ★ NEW YORK

Library of Congress Cataloging-in-Publication Data is available.

ISBN 978-1-5235-1210-2

Design by Jooahn Kwon
Illustrations by Irena Freitas

Workman books are available at special discounts when purchased in bulk for premiums and sales promotions as well as for fundraising or educational use. Special editions or book excerpts can also be created to specification. For details, contact the Special Sales Director at specialmarkets@workman.com.

Workman Publishing Co., Inc.
225 Varick Street
New York, NY 10014-4381
workman.com

WORKMAN is a registered trademark of Workman Publishing Co., Inc.

Printed in China

First printing February 2021

10 9 8 7 6 5 4 3 2 1

Dear Mom,

This book is all about YOU—your personality, your favorite things, and all the funny, weird, amazing stuff you do.

Even better, this is a book by ME!

If you're wondering why I needed a whole book to tell you all the reasons I love you, what can I say? Mom, you're a superstar!

Love,

_____

FIRST THINGS FIRST.

Your name is

_____.

But I like to call you

_____.

Your birthday is

_____.

You are _____ years old.

That means you're smarter than

_____.

Your favorite food is

_____.

Your least favorite food is

_____.

You love to cook

_____.

Your favorite color is

_____.

You are as tall as a

_____.

You smell like

_____.

I drew a portrait of you . . .

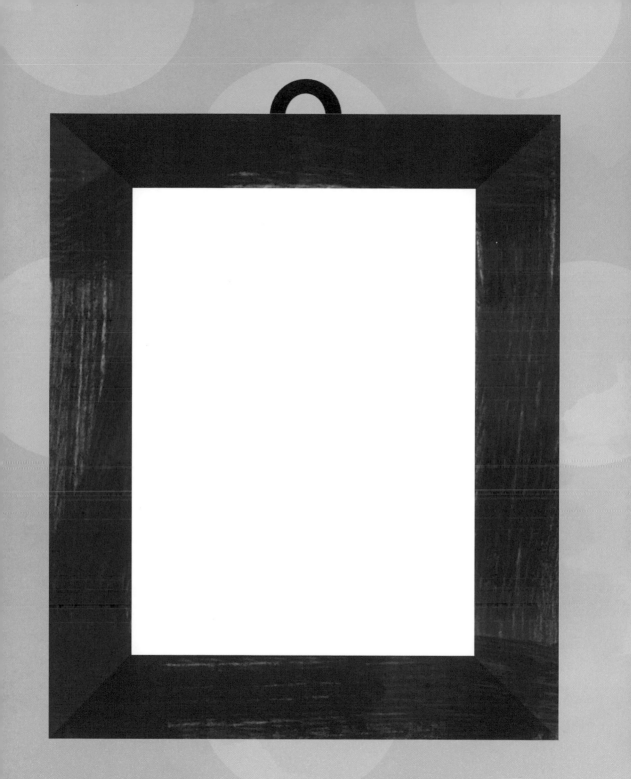

. . . and a portrait of me!

If you were an ice cream flavor, you would be

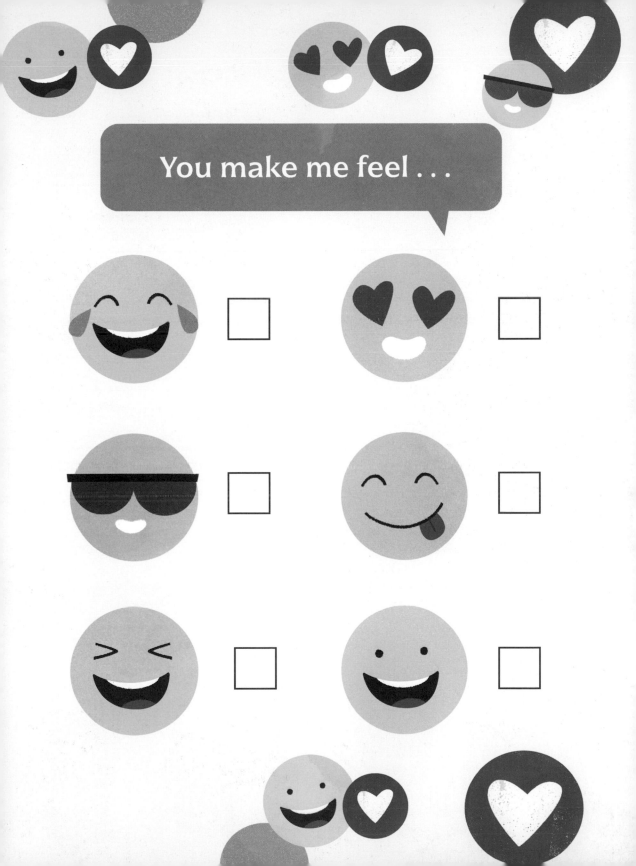

You make me feel . . .

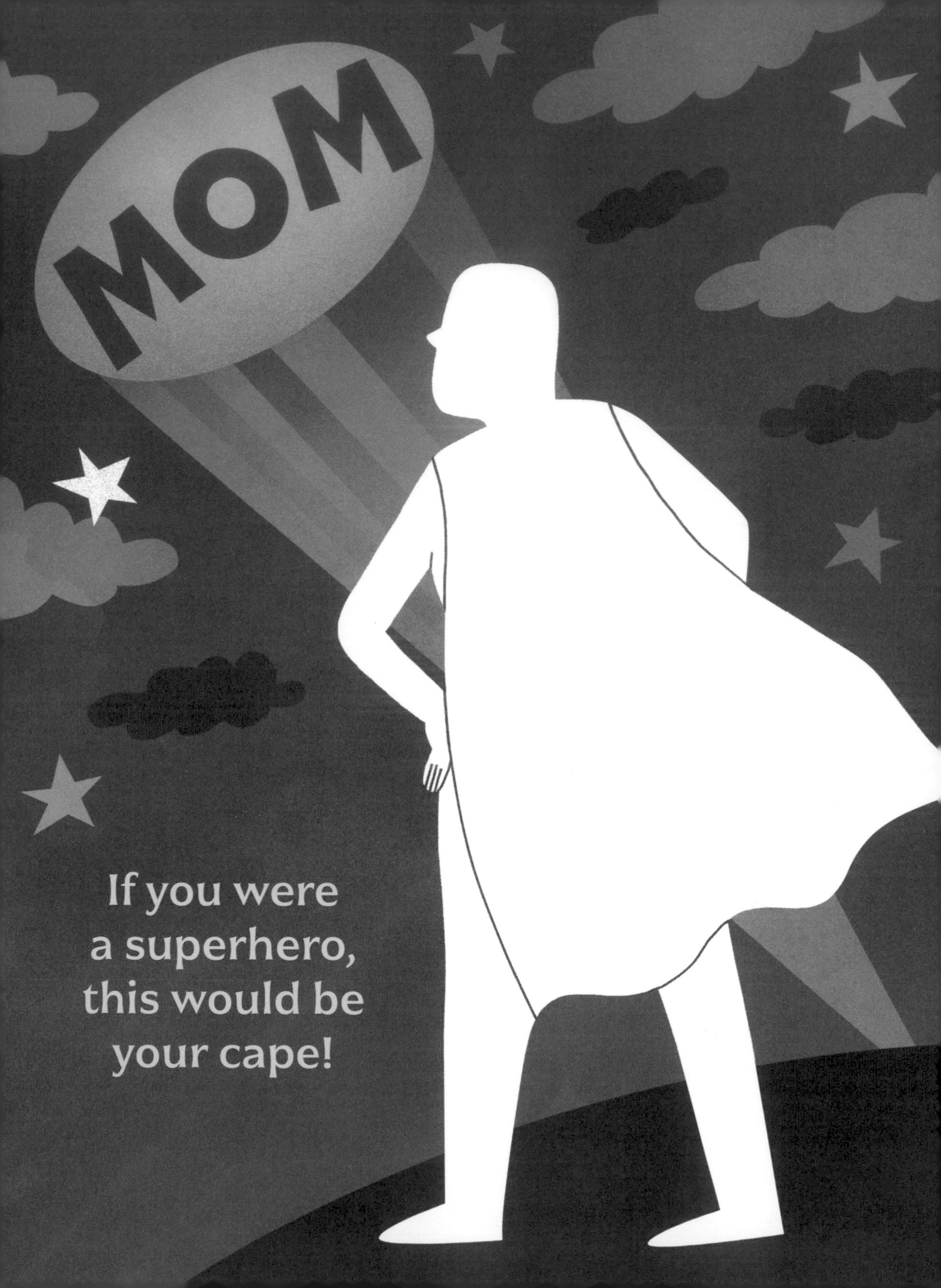

If you were
a superhero,
this would be
your cape!

My favorite thing about you is

_____.

Thank you for always helping me

_____.

Three things you do that make me smile:

1 _____

2 _____

3 _____

If I had a million dollars, we could

_____.

If you were a dinosaur, you would be a

_____.

Look, it's you!

My breakfast:

Your breakfast:

You can play the _____.

The two of us go together like . . .

☐ peanut butter and jelly

☐ socks and shoes

☐ cake and frosting

☐ the moon and the stars

□ summer and popsicles

□ music and dancing

□ zombies and pirates

□ a cat and a mouse

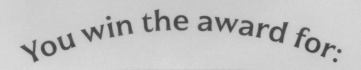

You win the award for:

I made you chore coupons!

Good For

Redeemed

Good For

Redeemed

Good For

Redeemed

Cash them in when you need some help.

If I had to describe you in one word, it would be:

But if I had two words, they would be:

If we were stranded on a desert island these are the five things we would need:

1 _____

2 _____

3 _____

4 _____

5 _____

I designed this super cool
tree house just for us!

You'll need this secret password to get inside:

Mom's Report Card

Subject	Grade
Math	_____
Jokes	_____
Cooking	_____
Science	_____
Fashion	_____
Dancing	_____
Hugs	_____

If you were an animal, you would be a

_____ .

Here's a picture of us on an intergalactic adventure!

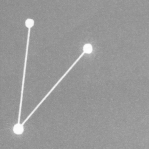
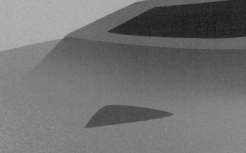

This planet is called _____.

I wrote a story about you. Want to read it together?

I drew a picture of my favorite part!

You always think about . . .

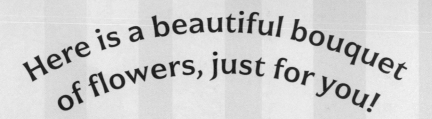

Here is a beautiful bouquet of flowers, just for you!

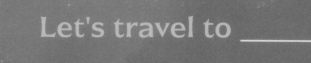

Let's travel to _____.

NORTH
AMERICA

SOUTH
AMERICA

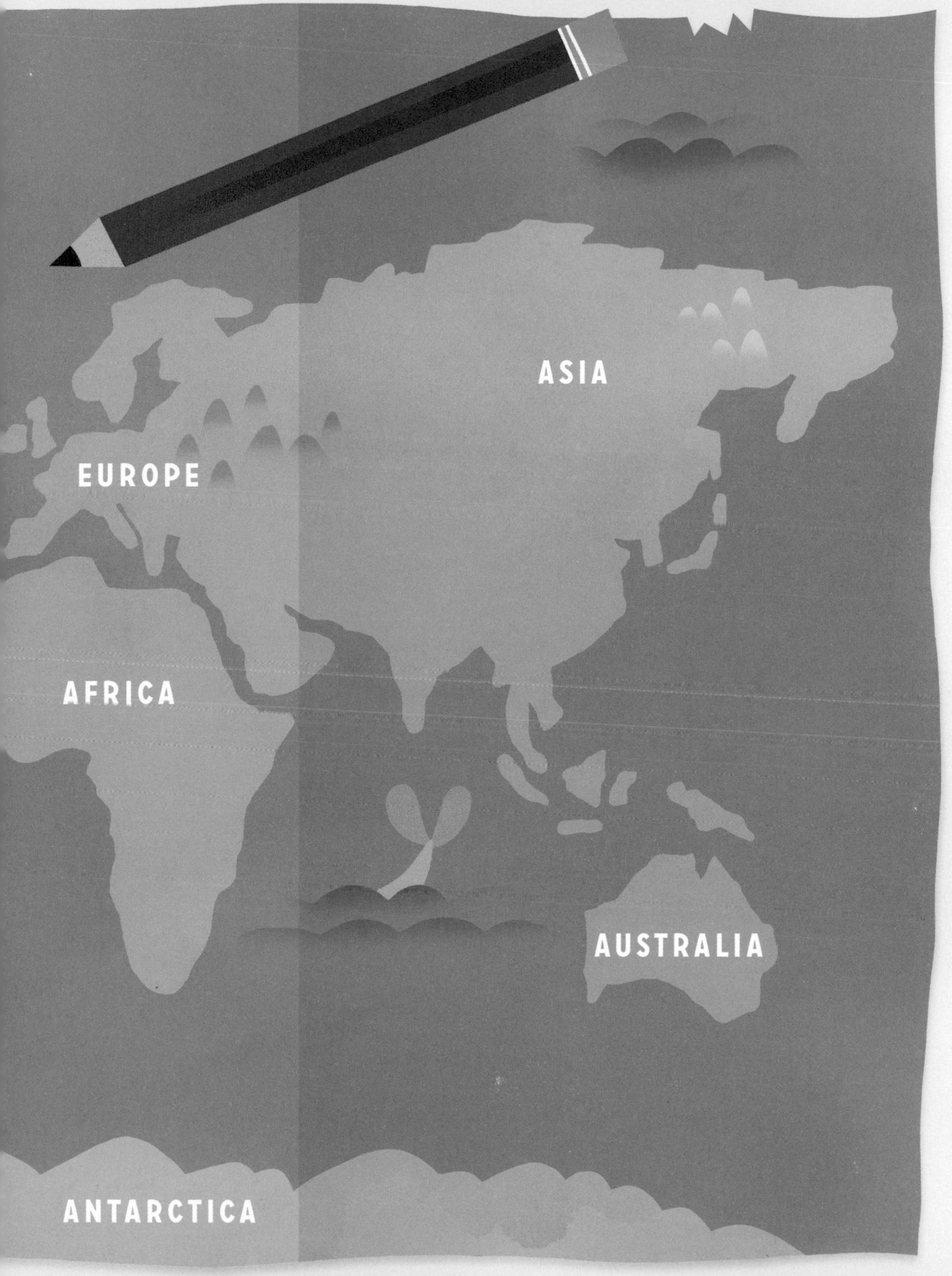
ASIA
EUROPE
AFRICA
AUSTRALIA
ANTARCTICA

Remember when we

_____?

That was so much fun!

Thank you for
teaching me how to

_____.

I baked you this delicious cake!

Can I tell you a secret?

On sunny days, we like to

_____.

On rainy days, we like to

_____.

You're really good at . . .

☐ cooking

HA HA HA!

tee hee!

☐ making me laugh

☐ juggling

☐ taking pictures

☐ driving

☐ gardening

☐ video games

☐ singing

☐ bowling

☐ magic

☐ arts and crafts

I made us matching T-shirts!

This is my favorite book
to read together.

This is how you looked when you were my age.

Mom, age _____

Look, I traced my hand.

Trace your hand too,
so we can high-five!

Our next pet should be a

_____.

I came up with a few new rules for our home. Here they are:

NEW RULES!

1.

2.

3.

4.

This is us,
having the greatest
adventure ever.

I love you, Mom!